FIRST STEPS

Word Fun 1

S. Cassin & D. Smith

Illustrated by A. Rodger

Collins: Glasgow and London

© 1980 C.E.M.A.
0 00 197012 7
First Impression 1980
Printed in Great Britain

All rights reserved. No part of this publication may be reproduced, stored in a retrieval system, or transmitted, in any form or by any means, electronic, mechanical, photocopying, recording or otherwise, without prior permission of the copyright owners.

My house

mummy   house   daddy

mummy   *house*   *daddy*

I like mummy.   I like daddy.

I like mummy.   *I like daddy.*

1 Talk about this house and compare it to your own. Talk about mummy and daddy.
2 Point to the words and read them. Write over the dotted words. Do the same with the sentences.
3 Colour the picture.

Further activities: Make a word box. Copy the five words on this page onto cards and keep them in the word box. Add words as you go through the book.

Helping daddy

daddy   mummy   car

I help daddy. I help mummy.

I help daddy. I help mummy.

1 Talk about the picture. Ask questions, e.g. What is daddy doing? Do you help your daddy?
2 Point to the words and read them. Write over the dotted words. Do the same with the sentences.
3 Colour the picture.
Further activities: Copy the new words onto cards. Make sure your child recognises them. Put them in the word box.

Little Miss Muffet

Little Miss Muffet
Sat on a tuffet,
Eating her curds and whey.
There came a big spider,
Who sat down beside her,
And frightened Miss Muffet away.

1 Read the rhyme and talk about the picture. Name the objects outside the picture. Ask questions about each one. Where does each go in the picture?
2 Write over each name.
3 Draw in each object and colour the picture.
4 Read the rhyme again and learn it.
Further activities: Make word cards for the names of objects outside the picture.

Words and pictures

house

mummy

flowers

spoon

bowl

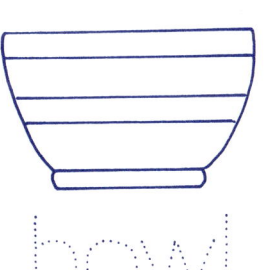

daddy

car

1 Talk about the page. See if your child can recognise the words in the list, which have all been met before.

2 When the words are recognised, join each word to its picture with a line.

3 Write over the dotted words and colour the pictures.

Further activities: Link words on cards with words on this page. Cover all but one word in turn. Always choose words which you think your child knows at this early stage, to establish success and confidence.

Waiting for a bus

girl   boy   bus   car   house

The girl is waiting for a bus.
The boy is waiting for a bus.

1 Talk about the picture. Ask questions, e.g. Who can you see in the picture? Where are they?

2 Write over the dotted words. Then read the sentences.

3 Colour the picture.

Further activities: Make word cards for the word box. Make sure your child can recognise the words.

The naughty dog

daddy   **house**   **dog**   **bus**

daddy   house   dog   bus

1 Encourage your child to tell a story based on the pictures. Ask questions, e.g. Where was daddy going? Why was he running? Was he pleased with the dog? How does the story end?

2 Read the words and write over the dotted ones.

3 Colour the pictures.

Further activities: Make word cards and put them in the word box.

Opposites

Mr. Lynn is very thin,
(palms close together)

Mr. Pratt is very fat,
(hands cupped together)

Mr. Cort is very short,
(hands near the ground)

Mr. Hall is very tall,
(hands stretched up high)

Mr. Dent is very bent,
(hands bent)

Mr. Wait is very straight.
(hands stiffly upright)

1 Talk about the people in the rhyme.

2 Read the rhyme doing the actions. Encourage your child to do the actions, while you read the rhyme.

3 Colour the pictures.

Further activities: Draw fat and thin people or animals, short and tall people or animals, bent or straight things.

Baking

mummy boy girl bowl bun

Mummy is baking.
I help mummy to bake.

1 Talk about the picture. Ask questions, e.g. What are they baking? How many buns fit in a tray?
2 Write over the dotted words. Then read the sentences and make word cards for the word box.
3 Colour the picture.

Further activities: **1** Make a picture of a kitchen – draw or paint it or cut pictures from magazines. **2** Find and read other 'baking stories', e.g. The Queen of Hearts, The Gingerbread Boy.

They go together

1 Talk about each line, identifying the objects. Ask questions, e.g. What is your favourite fruit? What don't you like? Ask which of the two objects on the right goes with each line. Give reasons why.

2 Write over all the names in each line and the correct one from the two objects on the right.

3 Colour each group of similar objects in a different colour.

Further activities: Make word cards and add them to the word box.

They go together

10

1 Talk about each line, identifying the objects. Ask questions, e.g. What is your favourite toy? Ask which of the two objects on the right goes with each line. Give reasons why.

2 Write over all the names in each line and the correct one from the two objects on the right.

3 Colour each group of similar objects in a different colour.

Further activities: Make word cards and add them to the word box.

Little Boy Blue

Little Boy Blue, come blow your horn,
The sheep's in the meadow,
The cow's in the corn.
But where is the boy who looks after
    the sheep?
He's under the haystack, fast asleep.

1 Read the rhyme and talk about the picture. Name the objects outside the picture.
2 Write over each name.
3 Draw in each object and colour the picture.
4 Read the rhyme again and learn it.
Further activities: **1** Make word cards for the word box. **2** Make Boy Blue's horn out of a tube from a kitchen roll and a plastic carton.

Animals

12

cow

horse

sheep

cow

pig

rabbit

sheep

rabbit

horse

dog

pig

mouse

dog

cat

cat

mouse

1 Talk about the pictures. Identify each animal and find its name in the list. Join each word to its picture with a line.

2 Write over the dotted words, and read them again.

3 Colour the pictures.

Further activities: **1** Make word cards for the word box.   **2** Find animal pictures in magazines and make an animal book. Help by printing the name of each animal under its picture.

All sorts

1 All the words on this page should now be familiar. Encourage your child to read each one.
2 Draw the pictures and write over the dotted words.
3 Colour the pictures.

The ice cream man

boy   **girl**   **house**   **mummy**

ice cream   **children**   **dog**

1 Encourage your child to tell a story using the pictures.
2 Read the words and write over the dotted ones.
3 Colour the pictures.
Further activities: Make word cards for the word box.

Me

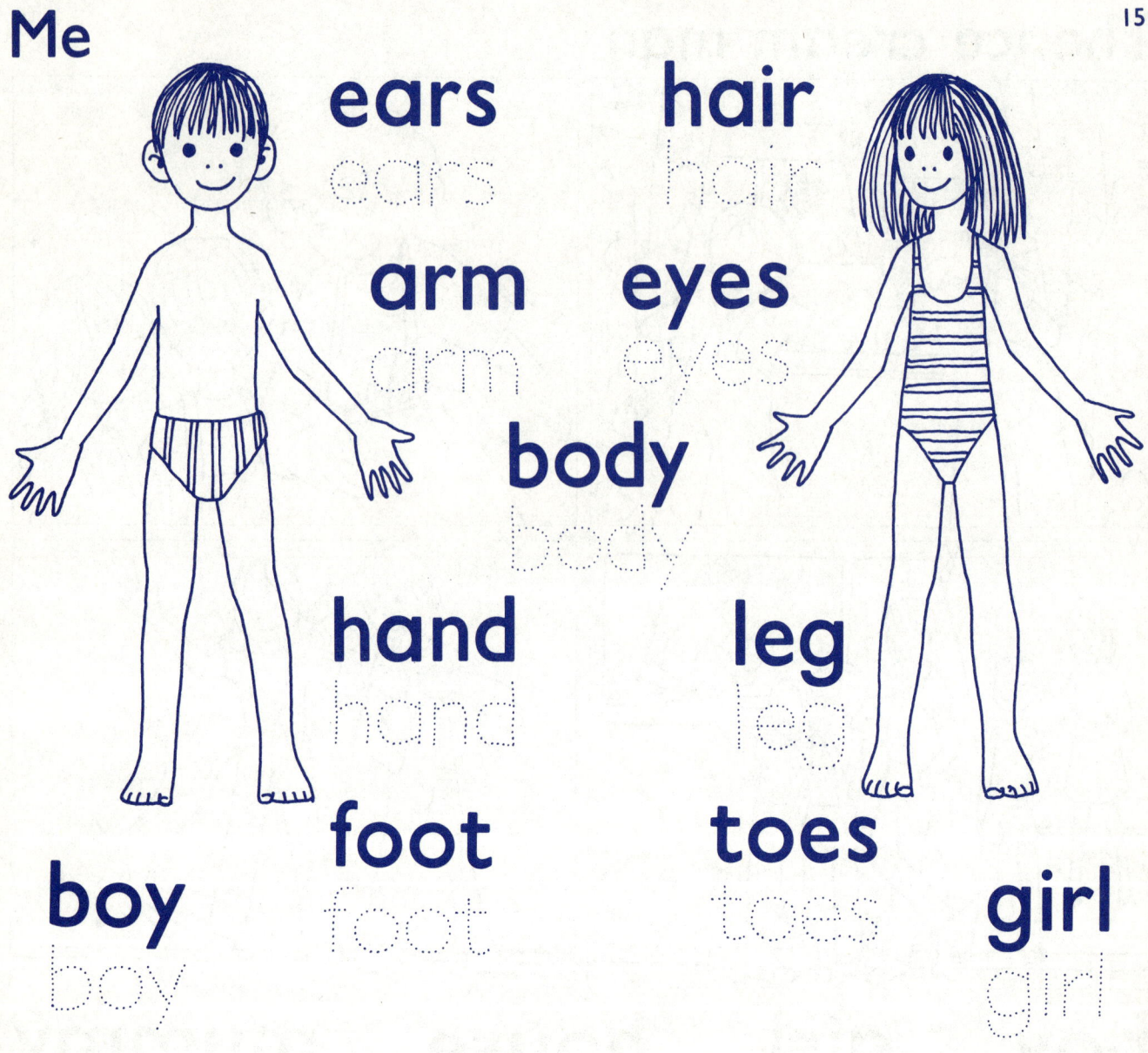

I am a _____. boy girl

I am _____. big little

1 Talk about the page. Name each part of the body, touching your head, hand, etc., as you name it.
2 Read each word and join it to the appropriate part with a line. Write over the dotted words.
3 Complete the sentences with an appropriate ending.
4 Colour the picture.

Further activities: **1** Make word cards for the word box. **2** Ask your child to lie down on a large sheet of paper (newspaper or wallpaper) and draw round him. Cut out the shape, colour and label the parts.

My bedroom

doll   car   bed   clock   cat

I have a bed.
I have a clock.

1 Talk about the picture. Ask questions, e.g. How is this different to your bedroom? How is it the same?
2 Write over the dotted words. Read the words, identifying the objects in the picture.
3 Read the sentences, then colour the picture.
Further activities: **1** Make word cards for any new words.   **2** Make a Bedroom Book with pictures cut from magazines, catalogues, etc.

The Old Woman in the Shoe

mummy   house   children

There was an old woman
   Who lived in a shoe.
She had so many children
   She didn't know what to do.
She gave them some broth,
   Without any bread,
And whipped them all soundly
   And sent them to bed.

1 Read the rhyme and talk about the page. Count the children. Ask questions, e.g. How many boys can you see? How many girls?

2 Write over the dotted words. Read the words.

3 Colour the picture.

Further activities: Draw or paint your house.

Rhyming words

1 Ask your child to identify the objects on each line. Read out the name of the first object. Ask him to listen carefully and to clap if any other name sounds like it, as you read the rest of each line.

2 Write over each word that rhymes with the first word in each line.

3 Colour the objects with similar-sounding names in each line.

Further activities: 1 Find words which rhyme with your child's name or with objects about you. 2 Make word cards for any new words.

More rhyming words

 **house**   **log**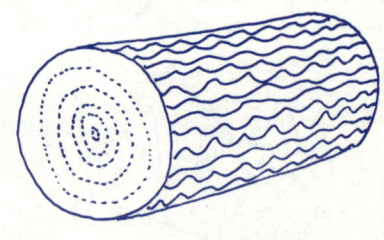

 **dog**   **mouse**

 **boy**   **sweet**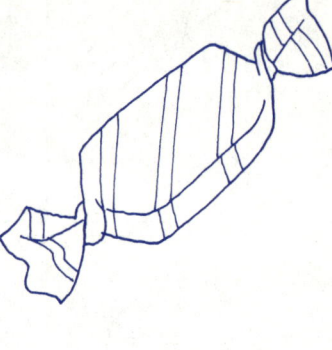

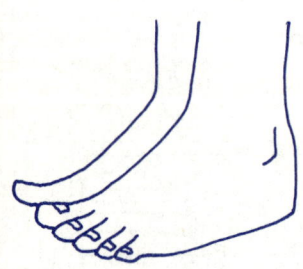 **feet**   **toy**

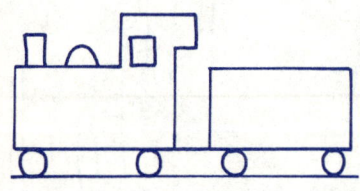 **train**   **rain**

1 Talk about the page, identifying each object. Read the words and with a finger trace a line from one rhyming word to its pair.

2 Write over the dotted words, and draw lines between pairs of rhyming words.

3 Colour the pictures.

Further activities: **1** Make word cards of any new words.   **2** Make rhyming snap cards with pictures cut from magazines.

The supermarket

1 Talk about the page and encourage your child to tell the story as it is illustrated.

2 Colour the pictures.

Further activities: Ask your child to retell the story while you write it in simple sentences. Then read it together.

Hickory Dickory Dock

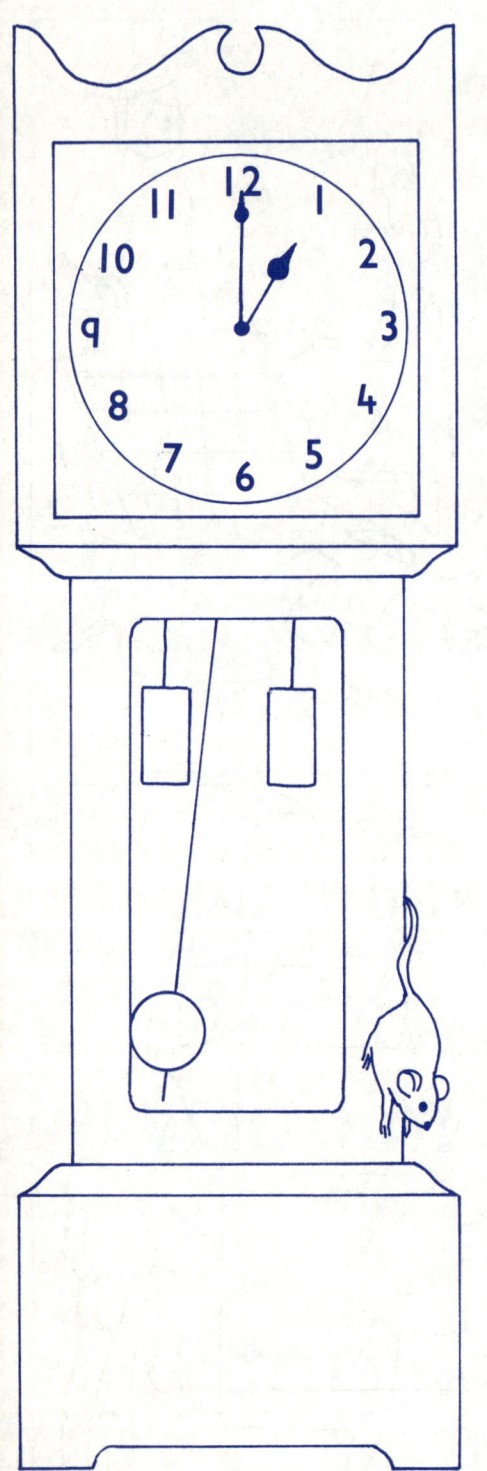

Hickory, dickory, dock!
The mouse ran up
 the clock;
The clock struck one,
The mouse ran down,
Hickory, dickory, dock.
Tick Tock

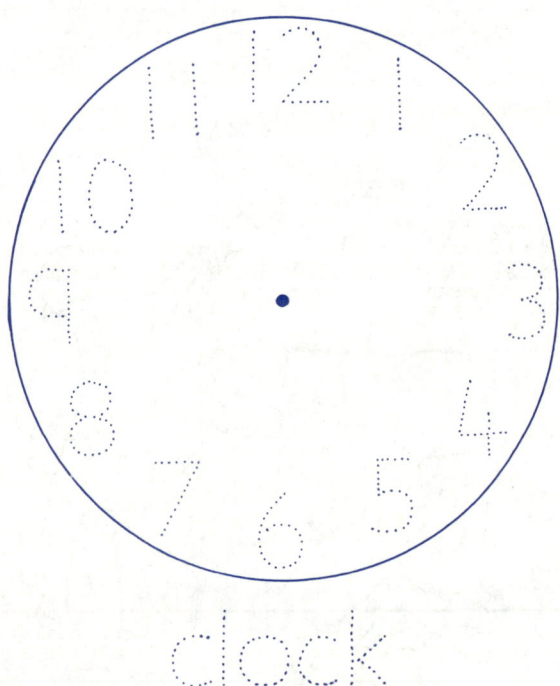

1 Talk about the page. Read the rhyme and talk about clocks. Count the numbers on the clock face. Ask questions, e.g. What time does the clock show? What time is it now?

2 Write over the dotted numbers on the clock face, and the word 'clock'. Put in the hands to show 1 o'clock.

3 Learn the rhyme. Colour the pictures.

Further activities: Make a clock out of card. Make the hands movable so that you can teach your child the time.

Time of day

morning
morning

midday
midday

afternoon
afternoon

night
night

1 Talk about the page. Look at the pictures and ask questions, e.g. When do these things happen?
2 Read the words and write over the dotted ones.
3 Colour the pictures.
Further activities: Make a book of My Day.

The weather

1 Talk about the page. Name each object and say what kind of weather it stands for.
2 Write over the dotted words and complete the sentence.
3 Colour the pictures.

Further activities: 1 Make word cards of new words. 2 Make a weather chart using these symbols, and note the weather each day.

What do we wear?

I like to wear _____.

1 Talk about the page and name each object. Ask questions, e.g. What do you wear when it's sunny? What do you wear when it's raining?

2 Write over the name of each object.

3 First with a finger, then with a line, join the correct object to the type of weather.

4 Complete the sentence and colour the pictures.

Further activities: Make a Rainy Day Book and a Sunny Day Book. Cut out appropriate pictures to stick in.

At play

boys   girls   children   friend

I like playing.
I play with my friend.

1 Talk about the picture.
2 Write over the dotted words and read the sentences together.
3 Colour the picture.
Further activities: Make word cards for any new words.

Food

ice cream
ice cream

sweets
sweets

sausages
sausages

chips
chips

egg
egg

crisps
crisps

I like to eat _____.

1 Talk about the page and name each object. Read the words together.
2 Write over the dotted words and complete the sentence.
3 Colour the pictures.
Further activities: 1 Make word cards for any new words. 2 Make a book about My Favourite Food.

Drink

27

cup
cup

milk
milk

glass
glass

orange
orange

tea
tea

mug
mug

water
water

I like to drink _____.

1 Talk about the page and name each object — first the drinks and then the containers. Decide which to use for each drink.

2 Write over the dotted words. Draw a line to link each drink with the most suitable container.

3 Colour the pictures.

Further activities: Make word cards for any new words.

I can read

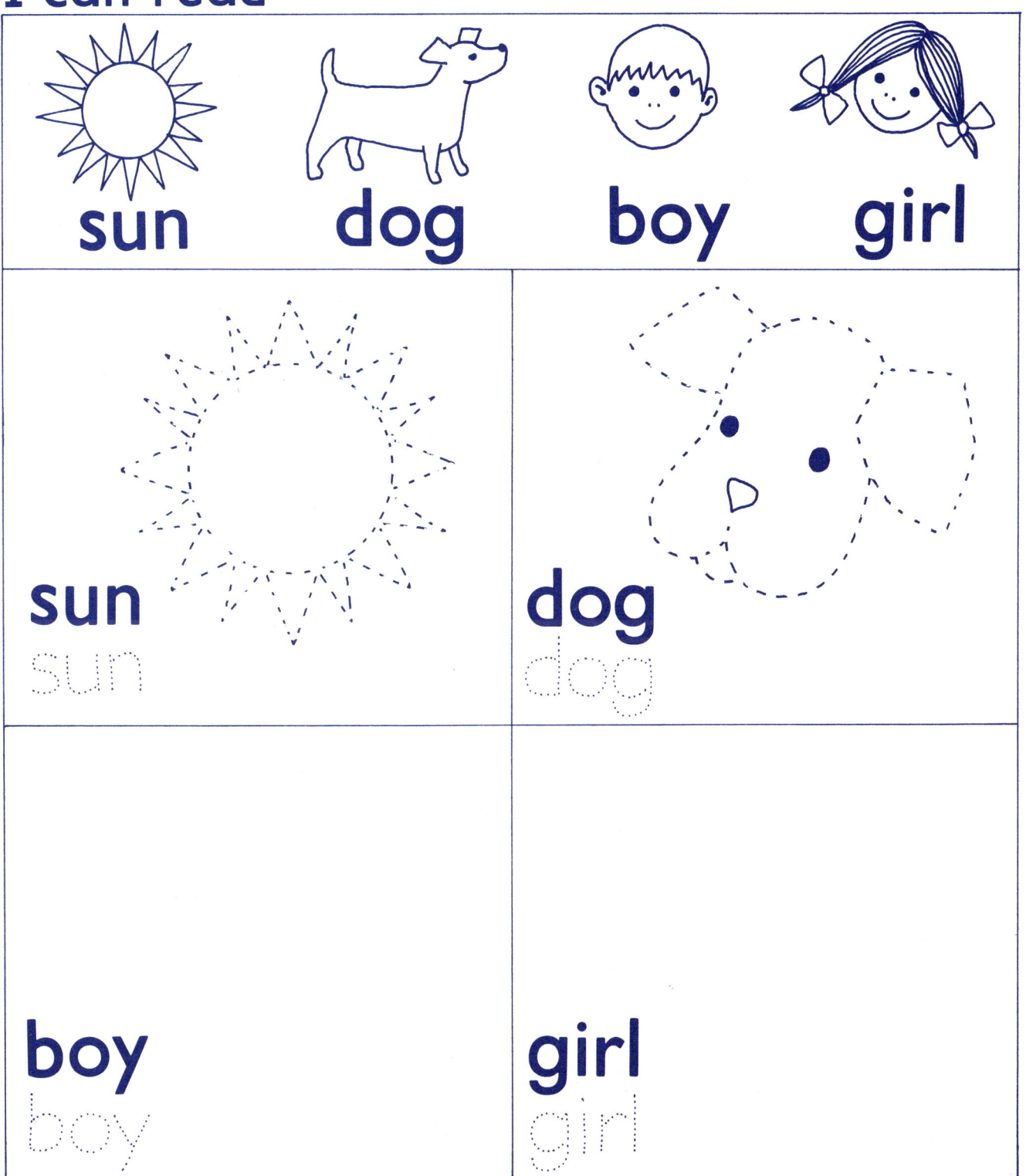

1 Talk about each picture in turn and read the words.
2 Write over the dotted words, then draw the boy and girl.
3 Colour the pictures.
Further activities: Go through the word cards to make sure your child recognises the words encountered.

Wild animals

tiger
monkey
elephant
camel
kangaroo
lion

1 Talk about the page and identify the animals. Find each name in the list and join it to its picture with a line.

2 Write over the dotted words, and read them again.

3 Colour the pictures.

Further activities: **1** Make word cards of new words. **2** Find more pictures of wild animals in magazines, and mount them on a large sheet of paper.

Humpty Dumpty

Humpty Dumpty
Sat on a wall,

Humpty Dumpty
Had a great fall.

All the king's horses
And all the king's men,

Couldn't put Humpty
Together again.

1 Talk about each picture in turn and read the rhyme.

2 Colour the pictures.

3 Read the rhyme again and learn it.

Further activities: Make a Humpty Dumpty out of egg shells stuck to an oval piece of card. Use scraps of material for his arms and legs.

A busy street

car   bus   girl   boy   lorry
mummy   daddy   dog   shop

I can see a car.
I can see a bus.

1 Talk about the picture. Relate it to any busy street scene. Ask questions about the bustle and the noise.
2 Write over the dotted words and read the sentences together.
3 Colour the picture.
Further activities: **1** Make word cards of new words.   **2** Draw or paint a picture of a busy street near your home.